Looking Beyond Behaviour to Make Connections

Margot McKinley

Results Press
Unit 229
#180, 8601 Lincoln Blvd.
Los Angeles, California
90045

www.theresultspress.com

ISBN-13: 978-0-9988905-7-9

First Edition

DEDICATION

I have had the honour of working and learning beside so many amazing people. I want to thank each of them for their part of my learning journey. From my teaching practicum with a teacher who was so ahead of the curve with her passion for connecting with and making learning real for kids, to the teachers who challenged me to be clear about my values, to the superintendents who saw something bigger in me than I saw in myself, to those who pushed me beyond my comfort levels and demanded more of me, to the amazing staffs I have had the privilege of working and growing with. I say thank you.

I also want to thank my first Grade 7 class who taught me so much about the value and power of connection...I love you all.

Ashley, thank you for helping me get through the final stages of this book and understanding what I needed to say.

I am eternally grateful to each of you who have made an impact on my life.

Prologue

Growing up, I always wondered why my teachers didn't realize I was in trouble. I wondered why someone didn't step up and say, "This child needs our help." Why was it that no one ever saw me? No one saw I was hurting, scared or confused.

This is why I've become so determined to *see* our students, to see the students who need to be seen and yet are rarely seen. The students who fall through the cracks of our systems are the ones who need us to see them the most. They're the ones who need to be heard and valued.

It is important as the trusted adults in their lives that we take time to understand what it is they need, to get to know them and to build a trusting relationship with them. This can make all the difference in the world for those students who are either engaged in socially unacceptable or harmful behaviours or are trying to be invisible and disappear. For some, that difference will keep them out of jail, help them find their full potential or even keep them alive. All it takes is for one person to make a positive connection to a student and make a lasting impact.

As a principal, I've been described as being a fierce warrior or fierce advocate for children. I am a defender and protector of children. My focus has always been what kids need. My belief is that kids' needs come first. They deserve and need to be heard and assured that they are safe and matter. Because when they know they matter, are safe and can trust you, they will begin to grow and learn.

In this book, I want to introduce you to some of the students I have known, that we all know. Some of these stories will sound all too familiar to you. These students are in every school. Every teacher, educator, parent and social worker has dealt with students like this and has wondered what to do and how to help. Some of my stories are about specific situations or circumstances, or they may be a combination of situations. Not all my stories are success stories. They don't all have happy endings, but they all have areas of growth and learning within them.

We all need to know we matter in life. I grew up with the belief that I did not matter, that no one saw me. It was with a fierce determination and stubbornness that I continued to grow and refused to succumb to that belief. Many others do not have the internal fortitude needed to make that move. The most important thing we can do in life is show people how important they are, that they matter to us and to the world. When we show others they matter, when we truly see them, that is where the magic happens.

As you read this book, I promise you, your perspective will change. It will have an impact on you and will shift the way you look at others. Every story may not resonate with you, but the ones that do will cause you to reflect on your own beliefs, practices and intentions about the kids with whom you come in contact every day. There are stories here that will touch your heart. You will become more intentional in the way you engage with students as a result of spending time reading this book.

It's not a new idea. We've seen the Maya Angelou quote everywhere. "Do the best you can until you know better. Then, when you know better, do better."

You will acquire an awareness as you read through these stories that will not only help you work and relate to your students who have experienced trauma, but you will also see how trauma impacts you personally. Your ability to see and understand reactions to trauma, whether it be your own or that of those around will increase, as will your ability to reduce its impact. This awareness and learning how to respond will reduce your stress and burnout and increase the joy and fulfillment you find in working with others.

I cannot find fault or blame my teachers for what they didn't know when I was in elementary school. I choose to believe they were acting with the best of intentions. Based on what I know, the education system back then did not provide opportunities to become educated about the social and emotional importance of learning--the focus was more on academics and behaviour. Thankfully, we are moving away from an industrial approach to education to one where we encourage individuals to be their best selves. We are coming to realize that when Maslow's hierarchy of needs is met, it is easier to accomplish and master Bloom's!

I'd like to challenge you to take some time with the *Stop and Reflect* at the end of each chapter and relate the questions to the people in your life, the ones you know and with whom you are dealing. Relate these stories to situations in which you have found yourself. I want to encourage you to practice, to try on some of the ideas I'm going to be introducing to you. These are not new ideas. They're not new concepts. They're nothing that you've not already heard before. It is my hope that these stories will inspire you to try again to reach out to those students who are struggling, to reach out to the most challenging students, to reach out and see those quiet students who are trying to be invisible in your classroom.

It is my hope that the lives you touch will be better because of that connection.

Happy Reading,

Margot

Relationships and connections can make or break a classroom environment, staff or team and has one of the biggest impacts on culture.

Chapter 1

Pieces of Your Heart

While reading this chapter, I'd like you to consider:

- Which children have you encountered who still hold pieces of your heart?
- What about them keeps them there?
- How have they impacted you?

I want you to think about those students who have stayed in your heart. Those kids who at times kept you up at night worrying about them. We all have those students who have broken our hearts. Something about each of them has left a piece of them stuck inside your heart.

A meaningful connection transcends words. A connection can reach beyond the unimaginable situations in which these kids are finding themselves. Maya Angelou said that, "people will forget what you said (or taught them), but they will never forget how you made them feel." They will never forget the connection you had with them.

So many times, there are students who come to school despite what is happening at home or in their lives. I had a Kindergarten student show up late to school day after day. When I asked how he got to school, he told me he had walked across busy highways by himself because his mom and dad were still sleeping. This five-year-old wanted to be at school because he felt safe, valued and loved there.

Sometimes school is the only safe place for children. There are many students who choose to come to school without the support of their families getting them there. Many times, they could have stayed home, watched TV or played on their iPads. However, these kids choose school, but they don't and won't learn from you if they can't connect with you. If they don't feel loved or cared for, they won't be able to engage. Just look at the choice they made to get to you. They left the uncaring situation to reach you.

This is particularly true for kids who have experienced trauma in their lives or for kids who are being raised by parents who have experienced trauma and don't understand how it impacts their children. Feeling as if they are liked and seen allows students to feel free to learn, to let their guards down a little, to let go of the need to protect themselves in order to trust. It is only when connection happens that you can genuinely teach them.

Think back to a teacher or mentor you had, someone who impacted your life.
What makes that person important to you?
Why did that person come to mind?

Most likely it was the connection you had with them, or more importantly, that they had with you. They saw you. They got you. Like I say they *had you* and you knew you mattered to them. You knew you were safe with them and they knew and accepted you for exactly who you were, not for who your parents were or what you had done or what had been done to you. Just for you.

Relationships and connections have the greatest impact. When you connect with others, they will work with you, learn from you and trust you. This includes everyone--students, teachers and colleagues. No matter what your title--principal, teacher, coach, mentor or student, when you come from a place of integrity, building connections based on trust and respect others will work with you, even when the task is challenging or less than engaging.

Relationships and connections can make or break a classroom environment, staff or team and has one of the biggest impacts on culture. I believe what is missing in schools, children's lives and yes, even in society, is a lack of the empathy that is developed through connectedness. If you don't have a relationship or a real connection with the student you are trying to teach or someone you are trying to influence, you are not going to fully succeed. You are not going to get that feeling of fulfillment or satisfaction because you positively impacted their lives. More often than not, those who need these connections the most are the very ones who are the hardest to connect with. It is often those kids who most desperately need you who push back, challenge you on every turn and defy you. You know the ones, those who are rarely absent, but when they are, the whole class notices and seems to go smoother. Connectivity comes from relationships, and relationships are built on connectivity.

You can, and likely have, attended numerous workshops, conferences and book clubs that focus on teaching and classroom management strategies. All the techniques and strategies in the world will not make a difference if you don't have a connection with your students.

Stop and Reflect

- So, the question becomes, how do you build a meaningful yet professional relationship with those with whom you are working?

NOTES

_____

_____

_____

_____

_____

_____

_____

_____

_____

_____

_____

_____

_____

_____

_____

_____

_____

_____

_____

_____

_____

_____

_____

The invisible student is a challenge to reach because they have likely already learned that adults are not to be trusted.

Chapter 2

The Invisible Kids

While reading this chapter, I'd like you to consider:

- Who are the students about whom you know very little?
- Which students have recently had a change in their behaviour? What might that change be communicating?
- When is it time to start really paying attention or being concerned about those quiet, or withdrawn students?

Some of the most difficult kids to reach or teach are those kids we don't notice or acknowledge each day. The kids are quiet and don't ask many questions. They are never in trouble, but when you stop and think about it, never really participate, either. They fly under the radar.

Sometimes we have that kid who usually asks lots of questions and demands attention suddenly go quiet. We forget about them after we have stopped being thankful they aren't bugging us so much, so we now have time to teach the others. When a student's baseline behaviour drastically changes in either direction, it is time for us as educators to start paying attention and to focus even more on keeping a positive relationship and line of communication open with these kids. These are the children who become *invisible kids*.

There are others who come into our classes and quietly appear to be doing their work. They never give us grief or disrupt the class. These kids are a dream to have because they *do* all the things we want them to. They quietly sit and listen, take out their books and don't wander around or ask anything more from us than we are already doing for them. These students will usually pop into your mind as you reflect on your day and you suddenly wonder, "Was she there today?"

I hate to admit it, but there have been times when I've sat down to write report cards and I am looking at a blank page...wondering what I can say about Johnny. In fact, I realize I don't know anything about him. With sinking stomach, I recognize I have not been aware of his learning. His assignments are missing, and I have nothing other than generic statements to write about him.

WOW...talk about a terrible place for a teacher to be! But if that is a terrible place for you, how do you suppose it is for the student? On the surface, they're just happy you are leaving them alone, not calling on them or putting them on the spot. But over time, what is the internal messaging they are receiving?

For a moment, if you will, consider that quiet, almost invisible student in your class. More often than not, they were not always invisible, and they are actually not invisible in other environments. When you see them outside of school, they are happy and bubbly. In parent conferences when a concern is raised, the parents are genuinely surprised, because they have never before seen this behaviour.

I know as a teacher, I used to feel defensive when parents would say this to me. I've come to understand that was my own defence mechanism kicking in. I have learned that this is a time to raise my curiosity, pay attention and seek understanding. Something has happened in their short life that has caused them to decide it is safer to be quiet and invisible in school rather than to reach out and be seen. It could be that there have been adults in their lives who've let them down. It may be that they have been embarrassed, left out or hurt by a peer and have lost their ability to trust and feel cared for or safe.

Many of our students have stories too heartbreaking to tell or sometimes even imagine. It is critical to recognize this but not to get hung up on the story. When we as educators hope to have an impact on students' lives and we stay focused on their life circumstances or on their stories, we'll begin to accept their behaviours without working with them to change them. I would never begin to suggest that we disregard their stories, but only hope to stress how important it is that we do not allow their life story to become the WHY of how we interact with them, create the expectations we have for them or provide the support for them to meet those expectations.

The invisible student is a challenge to reach because they have likely already learned that adults are not to be trusted.

They most likely will comply with whatever you ask of them when you are around but live the majority of time in their own worlds. This world may be in their mind, or it may be electronic in the form of gaming or other online community interactions. The only way to reach this kid is through a relationship. Take tiny steps with him, as well as how you treat and interact with those around him. These children are constantly watching to see if you are fair and kind to their peers. If you put a classmate on the spot or go back on your word with the class, you have a lot more work to do with this child. They don't trust easily, and they don't open up easily. More than likely they are afraid to get hurt or embarrassed in ways we may never understand. They have the same needs as other students, but they have learned it is easier and safer to be invisible. The more children disconnect with others, especially healthy adults, the more likely they are to engage in unhealthy activities or relationships in order to numb themselves or become more invisible.

Stop and Consider

- Invisible students need long-term support and reassurance in order to build a safe relationship and begin to open up. How do we accomplish that within the school day/year?
- The three components of trust are *Integrity*, *Transparency* and *Consistency*. Do others perceive you in the manner you think they are?

NOTES

_____
_____
_____
_____
_____
_____
_____
_____
_____
_____
_____
_____
_____
_____
_____
_____
_____
_____
_____
_____
_____

I believe kids want to learn and do better.

Chapter 3

The Ripple Makers

While reading this chapter, I'd like you to consider:

- What is it about the student who drives you crazy?
- What is their behaviour communicating?
- Are you missing their cues?

I want you to take a minute to visualize that student you have had in your class that MAKES YOU CRAZY! You know the one, the class clown or the perpetual socializer, or the one who asks so many questions it disrupts the lesson and others' learning all the time. You know the kid whose absence makes the class a pleasure to be in and your job so much easier.

Humour me...see that kid, say their name in your head and remember how they made you feel.

There are so many things we could talk about regarding this student, but first let me tell you a story. Allow me to introduce you to Noah. It was close to the beginning of my career in education. I was new and eager to learn. I wanted to show others that I was right for the job.

I was afraid to step on toes and didn't realize then how important it was to keep kids in the forefront of every decision and action plan made by schools.

Noah was the cutest kid. He always had a smile and was happy and eager to please his teacher. His parents liked to party, and party they did. Over the years, what had started off as drinking parties on the weekends escalated to drinking and using other substances regularly. With this lifestyle, it came as no surprise that not only did the dad lose his job, but his parents separated, as well.

As with most ugly separations, the kids often take the brunt of it, with parents fighting with each other in front of and about the kids. Noah got lost in the midst of the fighting and partying. He started to change in class, too. The transformation was so slow that at first it was unnoticed. As the changes grew and took hold, he morphed into a ripple maker.

He wasn't as happy anymore. He lashed out at his peers and did or said mean things to them. He no longer participated in learning, refusing to take out his books or ripping up his work. He never did his homework. From time to time, Noah ended up in the office. But more often than not, he would just end up in the hall. I couldn't disagree with the teacher. He didn't have the right to disrupt the other students' learning. So, naively, I thought it was right for him to sit in the hall and think about his behaviour and what he was going to do differently next time.

It was the classic, "You need to think about how your behaviour is impacting others."

As time wore on, Noah spent more and more time in the hall. In fact, he soon got a desk and chair in the hall where he was able to do his work. He was spending more time in the hall and less time in the classroom. I watched this change curiously. Was anything we were doing helping the situation? Were we even able to help?

As the years went by, Noah continued to be the problem student no one wanted in their class. Teachers explained that it wasn't fair to other students to have him in the class. He was too much of a disruption and the other students deserved to feel safe and have the opportunity to learn.

Let's fast forward to Noah's last year in our school. By this time, I was now the principal. I called him into the office to have a conversation with him about his experience at our school, to chat about his future goals and what paths he might take as he continued his journey. This was part of my responsibilities to do with every student before they moved on to high school. Together, we looked at the data that very clearly showed the decline in his academic progress, as well as attendance over the past three years. We sat looking at it, neither of us speaking.

Finally, Noah pointed to it and said quietly, "Right there. That is the year my mom and dad separated and everyone forgot about me."

Silence ensued. What more could be said?

We had failed Noah. The system had failed Noah and I had failed Noah. That was over 10 years ago, and the fact that I didn't look into the truth about what his behavior was communicating still haunts me.

I saw Noah the other day. I did not recognize him. In fact, I felt apprehensive when he approached me. His head was shaved, his face was covered with tattoos and he looked dirty and strung out. He walked up to me and asked if I was Ms. McKinley. Upon my nod, he said, "It's me, Noah." He told me he had a kid now, and that his brother had died in an accidental overdose. Noah had been in jail, and he told me he was between jobs. As suddenly as he approached me, he walked away. Just gone. Walking into a field and away. The sad look on his face is still with me.

I believe kids want to learn and do better. Unfortunately, their experiences often predict their outcome. They repeat behaviour that drives us crazy and subsequently cause us to lay down consequences which reinforce their feelings that they are a failure at school. So, after a while, they believe they are a failure at school and make up excuses about why they don't want to be there and why they cannot learn or are always in trouble. You see, once they perceive themselves as a failure, once they believe and own that label, they'll find ways to live up to the label to survive the day and the experience. They become what they think they are, or what they think we think they are.

There are so many kids like Noah in our schools. Those children who come into our classrooms whose reputation precede them. Those kids with whom we already know we are going to have trouble. Noah's experience at school was repeated failure that became his expectation of himself.

Our minds are made up about those kids, so that is the way we treat them.

Humour me if you will. I want you to do an experiment. This is for your information and interest only. It doesn't need to be shared with others.

Pick out a cute, popular, academically strong student in your school and watch all the adult interactions with that student. Watch beyond teacher interactions, but even how parents and volunteers interact or react to that particular student. Pay attention for a week or so.

Now, do exactly the same with a kid who is struggling academically, socially and emotionally. Count the number of positive or negative reinforcements each student receives in that week. And if you can see the difference, don't you think that discrepancy is likely way more obvious to the child? Do you think they don't know how others feel about them?

This takes me back to my senior year in high school. I was attending a private boarding school at the time. This was my second year there, but there was a new girls' dean. As I arrived at the dorm ready to start the new school year, filled with excitement for new opportunities and a chance for a great year, I was met by the dean. I will never forget the feeling I had opening that door and seeing her standing at the top of the stairs. Rather than welcoming me, she asked me if my name was Margot. Upon confirmation, her only reply was, "I have heard about you." In hindsight, I can honestly say that could have been taken any number of ways. But to my 16-year-old self, it was all negative. In my mind, she had issued me a challenge. She had let me know she was the new sheriff in town.

We all have preconceived ideas or first impressions about the students who walk into our classroom or school. We also give a first impression to students or staff when they first walk into our building. Those first few seconds or minutes can set the stage for the year. UNLESS you are paying attention. Let's say you messed up that first impression. It is easy to do without even realizing it. It is hard to undo a first impression, but it is not impossible.

Breaking down our preconceived notions and developing authentic views of our students are critical in developing meaningful connections.

This is so very important to keep in mind. It is why I wrote this book and why I share these stories with you, in the hope that I will inspire or motivate you to get back in there and *see* that kid who is struggling, that kid who annoys the heck out of you, that kid whose absence makes the day go by smoother in a different light. And that you will come away with some strategies to make meaningful connections.

Stop and Consider

- How much do you rely on first impressions or reports from previous colleagues on students, rather than taking the time to get to know them?
- Do you ever look beyond a student's behaviour?

NOTES

*How we treat and care for our students can
make a significant difference in their lives.*

Chapter 4

Desperate Times Call for Desperate Measures

While reading this chapter, I'd like you to consider:

- How do kids get to such a point of despair that they see no value in their lives?
- How do we reach kids to show them their value?

One in five people in Canada age 15-21 consider suicide. That is a truly terrifying statistic. That means in an average high school classroom of 30, there are six kids who have considered suicide as an option and may even have developed a plan. We know that the more specific they are in their plan, the higher the likelihood they are going to follow through with it. I am not talking about the kids who are having a rough day, had a fight with their mom that morning or who broke up with their boy/girlfriend. I am talking about those students who are slowly disappearing from us. Or the kids who are acting out so badly their behaviour is screaming at you to see their pain, to please see them and help them.

Let that sink in for a moment. Within your day, week, month or school year, you have the opportunity to connect with these kids and make a difference in their lives.

Which kids come to mind as you read this? Name them. Say their names out loud. (It is so important that you say their names and remember them while you are reading this.)

Building positive relationships, truly seeing and connecting with students is your single most important task as an educator. Without connections, kids cannot learn.

More frightening is the fact that while many kids have resilience, there are those who don't, and they especially need you to see them. Kids who have a meaningful and valued connection with a significant adult are more resilient and have a greater ability to work through their struggles because they know beyond a doubt that they have someone on their team.

Our broken students, the ones who need a support team, are most are often the hardest ones with whom to connect.

They have built an impenetrable wall in which to encase their emotions. Without having a positive role model with whom to connect, these children will seek connections elsewhere. Some of the places they may find relationships will be places we never want them to be, or with people who are not good for them to be with. Chances are that if you brush these kids off or are too busy, you will have lost the opportunity.

Sadly, many of these students turn inward. They may resort to self-harm and or ideation of death. This may turn into something we often label as *depression*. Even though we are not qualified to create that label, we feel the need to call it something.

Do we label kids to make ourselves feel better about not being able to help?
If *depression* or *lack of connection* is left untreated or is dismissed by adults as *another cry for attention*, or *Johnny always is saying that*, the problem may develop into more serious mental health issues or worse.

Once again, the problem is we are focused on the behaviour as something that needs to be fixed, not a method for the student to be communicating a need.

During my years in education, I've been frightened to see the increase in students who either consider suicide as an option or are engaged in self harm. What is equally, if not more startling, is the age of these students is getting younger and younger. I don't ever want to presume to understand or claim to be an expert on depression, mental health or suicide. I am not even close to being an expert. I can only speak about my observations and personal learning and experience.

What I very strongly believe is that how we treat and care for our students can make a significant difference in their lives. It is well documented that when kids like school or had at least one teacher who they believed cared for them it had a significant impact on the effects of the trauma they may have experienced in their lives. Having one teacher who connects with a student can save their life and change the trajectory of their life choices. One teacher who sees them, listens to them and makes them feel connected to the school makes the difference.

Stop and Consider

- How are you making a difference?
- Have you reached out beyond the behaviour?

NOTES

_____
_____
_____
_____
_____
_____
_____
_____
_____
_____
_____
_____
_____
_____
_____
_____
_____
_____
_____
_____
_____

Our challenge becomes how to build empathy in others,
to help them see and care about how they are impacting others.

Chapter 5

The Misfits

<u>While reading this chapter, I'd like you to consider</u>:

- The outcast student. That kid who just doesn't seem to fit in.
- Who are they?
- Do you recognize them?

Every time I saw Ichabod, along with his little sister and brother, my heart was sad. I felt a little angry, too. I first met the family a few years ago. Three kids, all struggling. They came from a place of poverty and a broken home. In fact, many broken homes. Their clothes often didn't fit right, they were always hungry and they didn't fit in well with their classmates.

As kids get older, they tend to become less comfortable around other kids who are different from them, and the more aware they are of those seemingly small differences. And these kids were different. They looked different, they had different names, their behaviour was different and their home life was definitely different than their peers.

Outward appearances were not the only way they were different. Each of them craved attention and wanted to be the centre of attention all the time. I found that I often made excuses for having to cut them short, or I would chat with them as I continued walking. They'd consume your time with endless stories and questions, and yet they struggled to socialize with their peers. They couldn't relate. They knew all the ins and outs of the latest games and most often lived in a fantasy- gaming world. They made up complicated games to play on the playground that mimicked or were an extension of the games they were playing online at night.

Home was often a state of chaos and mess. Not only was there not enough food, but there was regular violence and abuse--physical, emotional and verbal. This became their way of life, their norm. They didn't know any better. When they talked about it, they were very matter of fact about the fights or lack of food, or words their mom or her boyfriend of the day had said to them. Unfortunately, it was never quite enough to report them to Child Welfare.

As one could imagine, their lack of social skills led to all sorts of issues, including fights on the playground, angry outbursts in the classroom and an inability to see other perspectives or understand why others were upset. This often resulted in them being left out, made fun of and alone and sad.

So why do I share this story?
It's not new or unusual. As you spend more time in school systems, you'll often hear and see different versions of this story. It is a story we wish didn't exist, but I share it with you because it's important.

It is important for us to see these kids and to understand the trauma that has become so commonplace for them.

Most importantly, it is critical that we don't fall into the trap of complacency or simply joining in the masses who find them odd and annoying. Sometimes we have preconceived assumptions or generalizations which seem to give us permission to dismiss them, to look the other way or accept the way they behave and are treated or excluded.

Gabriella struggled with understanding social norms in her eighth-grade class. It didn't seem to matter what she did--no one wanted to hang out with her. She was always picked last when there were teams and she was excluded by other students during breaks and in class. The fact that she struggled athletically made her the brunt of some jokes in gym and out on the field. The only girls she REALLY wanted to be friends with were the so-called popular girls. They were a little clique of their own and wanted nothing to do with Gabriella.

Over the years teachers and councillors tried to help with friendship groups and different leadership clubs. There were other kids in the class who needed a friend, but Gabbie was determined only to be part of the one group she saw as popular. As time went on, it seemed as though it became okay for the popular girls to shun her and be rude. Office visits often resulted in plans that included Gabriella changing her behaviours without addressing the others. We encouraged her to be friends with other girls who also needed friends. Kids can be cruel, but over time the adults worked really hard to help her see that if she would just associate with others, she wouldn't experience these behaviours and attitudes from others. She was not only being bullied, but she was being blamed for the bullying, as well.

Our challenge becomes how to build empathy in others, to help them see and care about how they are impacting others. We must explicitly teach our students and the people with whom we interact to see that their behaviour is impacting the ways others are treating them.

When we look at the two stories shared in this chapter, many concerns come to light. What I would like to suggest is that there are gaps in social learning, and that as educators, we need to teach the skills students are missing to fill those gaps. It is NEVER a blame game! Mean, excluding or bullying behaviour is never ever acceptable. All students need to be taught how to empathetically interact in caring and kind ways. It is our challenge to set up the classroom/school environment in a way that reduces the triggers which may set students off, a classroom where acceptance and inclusion are the norm. This starts with you modeling and explaining expected behaviour. Be transparent, consistent and intentional with this.

Stop and Consider

- How do you teach empathy in your class?
- Do you recognize when you are being empathetic? Does it come naturally?

NOTES

_____

_____

_____

_____

_____

_____

_____

_____

_____

_____

_____

_____

_____

_____

_____

_____

_____

_____

_____

_____

_____

School is supposed to be the best time of a student's life.

Chapter 6

Mean Girls...is it just Finding Themselves?

While reading this chapter, I'd like you to consider:

- How do you connect with a mean girl?
- What do you think causes her to adopt this persona?

Mean girls. We all know them, have likely experienced them, have talked about them, read books about them or watched movies about them. We may even have been one of them. There's something so satisfying about watching those movies where the mean girls befriend the new girl, her personality changes and she turns into a mean girl. But in the end, she comes to her senses and remembers her values and the mean girls always pay. They pay through humiliation, rejection or some other lesson their peers provide for them.

Why are we fascinated with this scenario?
Why has Hollywood capitalized on these types of situations?

There are movies and television sitcoms based on the idea of mean girls. Most often, people find humour in their antics and are perversely satisfied when they get theirs or karma comes around in the end. If you have ever lived through this or been harmed by mean girls, you know it is neither entertaining nor fun. The reality is that these mean girls can cause lifelong scars. Some people carry these scars throughout their lives because of the cruelty they experienced by the carelessness, selfishness or insecurity of others, the stereotypical mean girls. There are so many situations where kids are mean and unkind to each other and they have no actual realization of the impact their words and actions have on the other person or on themselves. These mean girls indulge in a lot of gossip and enjoy mocking others. They feel good about themselves when they publicly ridicule people. The mean girls usually have a group of their own and look down upon everyone outside the group. They feel that they are superior to the other students in the school and have every right to humiliate anyone who doesn't live up to their standards.

School is supposed to be the best time of a student's life.

It is a time when life-long friendships and happy memories may be made. Unfortunately, for many students, this is not the case. We are all aware of the cliques which sometimes form, and that these can quickly become exclusive and unwelcoming to others who are different and don't seem to fit in. There are certain stages kids go through where they struggle with their identities. I can tell you from personal experience that I have watched many students struggle with who they are. It is during this time that they often go through stages of being mean. They display unkind behaviour to other girls and their friends in what appears to be a quest for power.

Lately it seems as though the easiest way for meanness to be spread is through social media. From the outside looking in, it appears there is safety in saying mean things from the security of your own room. Many of the students to whom I have spoken about why they use Snapchat or similar platforms tell me they feel like they can say things without being self-conscious about themselves, or they are afraid not to because they will no longer be in the loop, knowing what is going on. The majority of students who use Snapchat say they have been bullied, that their friends have betrayed their trust and that complete strangers have communicated with them.

Even those students who have been hurt badly and whose friendships and lives have been negatively impacted continue to use social media. They are afraid to withdraw from the social media circle because they're worried they will become the next target. They won't know what is being said within their peer group, and as a result, will be left out or fall behind. They're afraid they will go to school and not know what or who everyone is talking about because they didn't join in on the chat. What is more alarming from my adult perspective is that even though everyone supposedly knows who is being talked about, no one stands up to say that's wrong. Kids lose and make friends at a shocking rate based on the chatter that goes on via social media.

I asked several educators and parents what they thought some of the challenges were that students faced these days. The majority of people felt that overuse of technology for communication was leading to a breakdown in human relationships. It doesn't matter the age of the person--there often appears to be misunderstanding around email, texts, etc.

This is hardly a new phenomenon. However, the problem is what it is morphing into--the loss of human connection. We are losing the ability to communicate with each other because as we know, there is a lot more to communication than words on a screen. The evolution of texting has created a language of its own. Kids today are using Snapchat, Instagram and TikTok as their most common methods of communication. We are seeing more and more often that this language inserts itself into how children communicate with each other face-to-face. They don't realize they aren't building each other or even themselves up. Social cues are slowly disappearing during communication. This makes it harder and harder for students who struggle to be able to read a situation. As educators, we need to be able to be openminded and familiar with the ways in which our students are communicating, but equally important is the need to teach communication and conversation skills.

We have a hard time interacting as human beings because we are no longer a social society. Most people opt for convenience over connection, communicating via text, unlike years ago when people were forced to have face-to-face interactions. Communication and human interactions have become dehumanized. We are so busy that we would rather just pop off a message, ask a question or relay information through our computers or phones. We are losing the ability and the appreciation for developing conversations and spending time getting to know each other personally. It takes too much time. People are quite content to connect via technology rather than face-to-face. We have devalued the need for social niceties and personal contact. Kids are lonely and they don't even know it. They don't recognize that what they really need is face-to-face interaction.

How can kids recognize what they are missing when the adults around them are not modelling it?

One of the things that is missing, that has been disappearing over the past few years is humanness--the ability to feel and recognize empathy. Many seemingly private rants fail to take into account that everything we do has an impact. I cannot tell you how many students have said, "It's not a big deal. It was only on Snapchat," or TikTok or whatever platform they were using. They are disconnected from what they put out into the virtual world, yet they are deeply affected by what others put out there about them.

Think of the girl who is sent messages telling her she is ugly, fat, or worse yet, does not deserve to live. Think of the boy who is told he is useless or gay and is shunned in the hallways at school. These messages only serve to tear people down, and the person delivering the message feels powerful or popular protected by the screen.

Growing up and figuring out who you are and what kind of person you want to be is tough enough. All the pressures kids are facing these days compounds that struggle.

When we have a classroom community that values connection, supports individuality and encourages empathy, we are building resilience in students. We are creating awareness

Stop and Reflect

- How can the value of real lasting friendship be taught? What skills are missing when friendships dissolve over miscommunications?
- Have you ever considered that students who are exhibiting inappropriate or unacceptable behaviours may be missing social or emotional skills?
- How might changing your mindset affect the way you interact with these students?

NOTES

Our job is to create a safe place for students to learn the self-regulation skills they are missing.

Chapter 7

The Untamed

While reading this chapter, I'd like you to consider:

- Have you ever had a student who would go off like a ticking time bomb for no rhyme or reason?
- Did you ever consider that there may be a reason of which you were unaware?

I got called down to the Kindergarten room one day because one of the students was flipping over tables and throwing chairs. This is not typical five-year-old behaviour. As I entered the room, my first instinct was to ensure everyone in the class was safe. I asked the teacher to please take the rest of the children out to a different part of the school. Once it was just the two of us in the room, I tried to talk to the boy. I kept my voice calm and low and didn't approach him. I sat on a desk and remained still while he circled me like a wild animal. He growled and spat at me. I had never seen this type of behaviour before. Eventually, he calmed down. The first words out of his mouth were, "You know, I'm hungry." Absolutely not what I expected. To which I replied, "I didn't know that. Do you want to have a snack?"

I had just recently learned that kids cannot eat or drink when they are in a fight, flight or freeze mode.

So being able to offer a snack or juice box was a way for me not only to help restore some of the energy expended by the incident, but also to help his brain return to a place of calm and renew his ability to think clearly.

Like me, you are likely thinking low blood sugar may have aggravated this situation. There is definitely something to that, but that was not the end of the situation.

I asked Michael, "What happened?"

He told me he needed to finish his work before he could have a snack, so he missed snack time. This is not an uncommon practice in many classrooms. The hope is that next time Michael will finish up more quickly so he can have a snack, that he will make better choices the next day having learned his lesson today.

Unfortunately, that was not the case. This was not the lesson that needed to be learned. I asked his grandma, with whom he lived, to please have a pediatrician see him and do some testing to see if there were any physical concerns of which we needed to be aware. Because you see, this had become a very regular occurrence for Michael. I could almost guarantee, particularly on Monday, that I would be called to that class. I won't give you all the details of how many times I was hit, kicked, spat on, screamed at, etc. by this tiny, confused boy. There were days I would go home exhausted and bruised.

The more I learned about him, the more it became crystal clear that he was in a heightened state of alert most of the time. He didn't know what it was like to let his guard down. As I learned more about his family history, I began to understand more fully. Family history can explain a lot, but we cannot use it as an excuse for behaviour, though it may be an explanation for it.

Like so many others, Michael witnessed domestic violence on a regular basis. Both his mom and dad struggled with substance and alcohol abuse. There were concerns about money and making ends meet. Michael ended up being removed from his home and was now living with his grandmother. He got to go home to see his mom on weekends. Suddenly, the Monday morning episodes started to make sense.

As we got to know him and build trusting relationships with him, baby-step by baby-step we were better able to meet his needs. We were better able to support him while still holding our expectations high.

Did his story break our hearts? You bet it did! But imagine what might have happened if we had made concessions for his behaviour rather than finding out what he needed, what we do to help him to learn and practice and integrate into his daily life. Our job was to create a safe place for him to learn the self-regulation skills he was missing. It was not to punish him into behaving, because punishment didn't work. We needed to provide a place he could practice and learn about regulating his emotions and behaviour. This was the only way to build resilience within him.

Stop and Reflect

- How can you find balance between meeting all the needs of the students in your class or school?
- Identify one step you can make this week to structure your class in a way that takes care of students' personal needs while maintaining a learning environment?

NOTES

_____

_____

_____

_____

_____

_____

_____

_____

_____

_____

_____

_____

_____

_____

_____

_____

_____

_____

_____

_____

_____

_____

Our job is to offer hope for a brighter future.

Chapter 8

The Excuses

While reading this chapter, I'd like you to consider:

- Have you ever dismissed a student's behaviour because of their story?
- Do student's backgrounds and family histories impact your perspective of them?
- Are you aware of your perceptions?

Sometimes we get so caught up in a student's history or family story that we end up making excuses for not reaching out and meeting the needs of him or her. We say, things such as, "Oh, her mom is abusing substances," or, "She is an alcoholic," or, "She has a new boyfriend in the house every month." We say things such as, "Oh, her dad ... blah, blah, blah..." You know the stories, the rumours and the histories about which we talk.

As we retell and recount these familiar family stories, we play a trick on our minds. We pretend we are building relationships, caring and understanding. We tell ourselves that we know this child's history, so therefore we are treating them with that in mind.

This is often the most unfair thing we can do to a student.

We judge them by their family or life circumstances. We may even create learning plans and goals which limit them in the belief that we are being supportive and caring.

This is not to suggest even for a moment that it is not important to understand the family dynamic and situation, as it does explain some of the behaviours and challenges the student may be facing. We cannot disregard or ignore that. However, what often happens is that we get trapped or stuck in the storytelling and never move into the solution or problem solving aspect. We become despondent and forget that as professionals, our job is to create an action plan which will move the students out of and past their life experiences and offer them more for their lives. Our job is to offer hope for a brighter future.

We get so caught up in being *understanding*, blaming parents or life circumstances for where the students are and for their behaviours, that we lose sight of the fact that our job is to offer high levels of support and caring to that student in order to help them reach maximum achievement.

In essence, we use their current or past circumstances as our excuse for not helping them. Sometimes we tell ourselves that we are being caring while we lower our expectations for their behaviour or academic achievement. We think we're being sensitive to their needs by not pushing them or asking too much of them.

And yes, I know I am likely stepping on some toes right now, but that is the point--to become uncomfortable with being complacent. The *why* becomes an excuse rather than being a building block to establish understanding from which we can construct an educational program that meets the student needs, a plan which empowers them to gain the tools, strategies and education they deserve. We end up failing our most vulnerable students because we have made a pile of excuses about why they cannot possibly be expected to be successful.
The worst of it is that we have done this from a place of love, nurture and caring, from a place of our best intentions. In order to teach, we need to know where a student is currently, as well as where they should be. It is our job to help them fill in the missing pieces, to teach them the skills they are currently lacking. We know how to do this when it comes to academics. What we need to learn is how to use this same level of intention when teaching social and emotional skills,

resilience and self-regulation. This is the transparency of learning and the reason behind building connections. Without this connection, we cannot discover, identify or help students grow in these most important areas.

Stop and Reflect
- Take some time to reflect on the struggling students in your class. Write down your expectations for each of them.
- What are the excuses for their behaviour or learning?
- Now, be honest, are you selling them short because you don't want to add stress or pressure them?
- If the answer is yes, what can you do to support them by identifying where they need to be and the steps, maybe baby steps, needed to help them achieve those goals?

NOTES

_____

_____

_____

_____

_____

_____

_____

_____

_____

_____

_____

_____

_____

_____

_____

_____

_____

_____

_____

_____

_____

_____

With practice, kids can learn to slow down their anxious brains, and teachers can learn to help them.

Chapter 9

When Labels get in the Way

While reading this chapter, I'd like you to consider:

- How often do you categorize students by labels?
- Do you recognize when you are labeling students?
- Do you ever look beyond the labels?

Emily suffered from anxiety. At least I thought she did. Her parents said there was nothing wrong with her and she just needed to behave and do her work. She was expected to follow the rules and not get into any trouble. Emily had a deep need never to disappoint her parents and often said she felt like a failure because she had made a mistake somewhere along the way. I cannot tell you the multitude of times Emily was in my office, out of control and shouting that she was a disappointment to her parents, and she didn't deserve to live. She said she should just crawl into a ditch and stay there because she was a disgrace. Trust me, I had many opinions about Emily and her family. She had an older sister who was withdrawn and quiet and a younger brother who cried a lot over just about everything. I knew some of her family history but not all of it. I knew her dad suffered from depression and was being treated for mental illness, and I knew he struggled to leave the house.

I had a such soft spot for Emily. When she was in kindergarten, I decided I would be her defender, her advocate. I would make sure the school provided her with what she needed in order to be successful and happy. I wanted to protect her from those things that caused her such stress. You see, in her early years, her teachers didn't know what to do with her. They were unable to understand or connect with her, so she spent a lot of time in the office with me. She became disconnected from her class. Other students were frightened by her outbursts, and she was never able to find a friend or develop those friendship skills normally learned in Kindergarten. She never understood why she wasn't allowed to finish one activity before moving on to the next or why, when she wanted to start over because it wasn't good enough, the teacher wouldn't let her. She would argue with me that she should be able to do it again because it needed to be perfect--and was that so wrong?

While I had a soft spot for Emily, I was not equipped with the knowledge I needed to help her. I did the best I could with what I knew at the time. I was able to give her a safe space to work and let her stay with me until she was calm. Regrettably, I didn't have the skills to help her learn about self-regulation, which in hindsight is what she needed to learn about and practice. I worried about her and I began to talk to professionals in the district about her. I developed strategies that might help her.

Her parents did not see the problem or think or admit that there was anything unusual about her behaviour. Their only concern seemed to be that she didn't get into trouble or that they not get a phone call about her. They refused to seek outside help, let us administer any tests or engage her in any programs that would make her appear different than the other kids in her class. At that time, I felt like the responsibility to help Emily was squarely on my shoulders.

One day when she was having a particularly bad day, she asked me why no one was helping her. Couldn't we see she needed help and something was wrong with her? Why wasn't I helping her? It almost broke my heart. As she ranted on and on, her tirade became louder and louder, her breathing came faster and faster and I could see her emotions were escalating fast. I happened to be wearing a top that had a ruffle down the front. Imagine my surprise when she reached out and took that ruffle and started rubbing it between her fingers. The most amazing thing was that she began to calm down.

What a lightbulb moment for me! Not anything to do with me wearing ruffled tops, but that Emily needed to have something tactile in order to calm her nerves and reduce her stress. The other things I worked on her with was to calm and regulate her breathing. One of the simplest tricks I have come across, and again, this is not my discovery or creation, but I can tell you that it works because once I started to use it with Emily, I realized there were other students in the school who would also benefit from it. I would put my hands on her shoulders, tell her to look only at me and not worry about anyone or anything else. I would reassure her that she was safe. All that mattered right then was me. Standing there holding eye contact, I would make Emily match my breathing. In and out. I would count, and she would breathe with me. Once she was focused on my breathing, we transitioned into making the *S* sound, I would say, "Take a deep breath in and push it out through your teeth. Make your hiss last as long as you can."

The act of breathing out, "*Sssssssssssss*," worked to calm and focus her every time. EVERY time. Sometimes she would say, "Do I have to?" But it always worked. In her heightened state, she would often not want to cooperate with me, but she would always comply. Through this simple technique, Emily learned that even if I wasn't there, she could calm herself and work through her stress. She was beginning to trust and use the strategies I had modelled for her. I don't want to oversimplify these easy strategies. They are far from what Emily really needed. But this was a tool that worked for her when she needed to calm down, when her world seemed to be out of control for her.

You see, I don't know what triggered Emily. I don't know what was currently or had gone on in her life to cause this reaction from her. I had all sorts of theories, but none of them mattered. In fact, those theories got in the way of us helping Emily, because we made assumptions about her and her family. All that really mattered was that we do whatever needed to be done to help her to learn how to gain control of her emotions and be able to function in a happy manner.

Kids who have gone through any type of trauma don't necessarily know what is wrong with them. They don't know what things trigger them. They're always on guard. They're always on high alert in case they need to protect themselves. So, while I knew Emily was safe, I needed to lay my hands on her shoulders with some pressure and make her focus on me so I could tell her she was safe, that I was with her and she was able to calm herself because she knew she was safe. The slow breathing allowed the adrenaline to gradually leave her body and allow her to think for herself again.

It was always pretty obvious when Emily was struggling. Other students struggle with fears, phobias and anxiety in the classrooms in a variety of ways. Often, they are not nearly as loud, demanding or obvious as Emily was. Anxiety in students can exhibit itself in a number of different ways. They may withdraw, feel sick (I know one student who vomits when he is nervous) or have a hard time speaking or moving. They may have outbursts and refusal to do their schoolwork. Anxiety is difficult to pinpoint because it can present in so many different ways. Neurologist and former teacher Ken Schuster, PsyD, suggests that the one thing all these symptoms have in common is the neurological effect. Anxiety "tends to lock up the brain," making school hard for anxious kids. Many anxious children struggle internally without actually seeking help from the classroom teacher. They might appear to be "quiet" or "disengaged," but really, their brains are consumed with worry.

Kids who are worried and anxious aren't doing it on purpose. They aren't being defiant or withdrawn on purpose. In fact, most likely, they wish they could be doing anything other than feeling and acting the way they do. But the nervous system acts automatically, especially when it comes to worry. That's why phrases such as *just relax* or *calm down* aren't helpful. However, with practice, kids can learn to slow down their anxious brains, and teachers can learn to help them.

So often we find ourselves in situations similar to the one in which I found myself with Emily. We see that our students have needs which appear to go beyond our ability to deal with. The system seems to be failing them because of a lack of services and qualified people to help. There are a million reasons over which we can lament about how the needs of our students are not being met, and how teachers are wearing so many hats that they barely have time for teaching anymore. These reasons, the lack of resources and frustrations, are real. I hate it when people say this, but we are where we are, and we are here right now. We have the choice of throwing our hands in the air, pointing fingers and doing nothing, or we can do something. We can step up and do the best we can with what we know for our struggling students.

It's essential to develop a positive relationship with your students.

Commit to doing regular check-ins with them to see what is working for them, what they need and what they may be struggling with. It takes time and patience to develop strategies which will best help them, but once you establish a trusting relationship with them, you'll be better able to meet their needs and help them thrive in your classroom while learning to manage their symptoms. Making small concessions on your part can make a huge difference in their mental health and success at school.

Stop and Reflect

- Have you ever actually noticed your own breathing? When you pay attention to it, how does it change?
- Do you see signs of anxiety in your students?
- What are some self-regulation skills or practices you use in the class or at home to help someone regain or maintain control of their emotions?
- At what point do you seek support?

NOTES

Showing students that you're not perfect helps them understand that it's okay to have flaws and imperfections.

Chapter 10

The Witty Avoiders

While reading this chapter, I'd like you to consider:

- Have you ever had a student who uses their wit to avoid their work?
- How often have you become frustrated with the interrupting humour and removed them from your class?
- How do you measure improvements in student behaviour and engagement?

Jaxon was new to our school. He had a twinkle in his eye and was always the center of action and fun. What drew others to Jaxon was his quick sense of humor, his ability to include everyone and his seeming uncaring for what the adults in the building thought. I enjoyed joking and chatting with Jaxon. He was polite and fun and always seemed to want to chat. Not only was Jaxon new to our school, but he was new to a group of peers who had grown up together, a group who had attended the same school for the past six years and knew all the staff, rules routines and norms.

As time went on, I realized that Jaxon never got his homework done, that he was often the instigator in mischief around the playground and he distracted his peers in class, so everyone's learning was impacted. The classroom teacher was frustrated and didn't know what to do. You see, Jaxon was one of those students who would talk to anyone and everyone. He included everyone and attempted to be everyone's friend. Moving his seat around didn't help.

The teacher resorted to sending him out of the classroom to think about his behavior. While in the hallway he would wander and visit and smile and help. There were many times when I saw Jaxon helping other teachers or younger students. Whenever I would talk to Jaxon, he would acknowledge that he knew that he needed to be quiet and to focus and that he was stealing learning from other students. Every time I talked to him, he promised that he would go back to the classroom, pay attention and do what needed to be done.

Jaxon was super likable. It soon became evident that Jaxon would do anything to avoid work. As the year went on and the pressure increased, Jaxon became less pleasant and more belligerent. I spoke with Jaxon so many times that I'd begun to lose patience with him. I didn't understand why someone who seemed to know how to behave, appeared to understand the expectations and who wasn't struggling socially refused to engage in the classroom. He wouldn't do his work and he had many excuses, such as he forgot his work at home or he didn't know it was due and more. It got to the point that every time I saw Jaxon, I became annoyed. Jaxon started to be less friendly to me and less likely to speak to me in a respectful manner. He knew I was frustrated and he gave me exactly what it was I was expecting.

In an act of desperation, I asked the vice principal to interview Jaxon and me. In the interview, I said I was not the principal but that I was another human being who needed to sort out a problem. I made myself equal to Jaxon and not above him. In that interview, the vice principal followed the questions outlined by IIRP. She asked us what had happened and what was happening. The vice principal also asked how that made us feel. At first, Jaxon was hesitant, but as he listened to my honesty, he became honest and open, as well. The vice principal asked us five questions:

1) What was happening?

2) What were we thinking at the time?

3) What had we thought about since?

4) Who was impacted?

5) And finally, what needed to be done to fix the problem?

Each of us answered those questions, and as we answered, I came to a better understanding of Jaxon. Not only that, but he had a better understanding and appreciation of me. When it came to the part about how we might fix this problem, I discovered that Jaxon had missed a lot of school. He didn't feel like he belonged, and he was ashamed that he was behind where he should be academically. I should've known this, but I didn't. I asked Jaxon what he needed and if he would be willing to work with me privately in order to get caught up with reading and mathematics. Jaxon agreed.

It took courage for me to be vulnerable, both with my VP and with a student.

Being vulnerable in the classroom can promote deeper thinking, may strengthen your relationships with students and will prompt more authentic responses.

Showing students you're not perfect helps them understand that it's okay to have flaws and imperfections. Students know when we are being our authentic selves. Sometimes they can see through us likely better than we can see ourselves. Vulnerability leads to safety, which in turn leads to a connection that makes a difference.

This wasn't rocket science or a new method, but the relationship that Jaxon and I had after that interview was different. I was being held accountable to honor the promises I'd made to Jaxon and I had a better understanding and acceptance of his behavior. He had a better understanding and acceptance of the school expectations for learning and behaviour. We didn't agree to lower expectations in that meeting. Rather, we discovered skill gaps and devised a plan to fill those gaps. When I found out that he moved often and that his mom and dad fought all the time, I discovered his home was not a happy place. When Jaxon came to school, he didn't want any pressure. He couldn't handle any more pressure. What he needed was a caring place where he could be happy and carefree without feeling pressured.

Getting to know Jaxon better allowed me to have high expectations of him. It also made him realize that with these expectations I would also give him the support he needed. He saw me as a human being who cared for him rather than the principal who was looking to see if he was in trouble again. He knew I was there for him and I actually cared for him and would help him in any way I was able. Such an easy method, about ten minutes and a world of difference. I was able to tell Jaxon how I felt in an affirmative and positive manner. He was able to express his feelings in a safe zone because I was another human being. I was a person who cared enough to take the needed time to work through this WITH him. I wasn't doing something TO him. I wasn't making or accepting excuses for his behaviour. He and I worked together to sort out the issues we were having and that made a big difference in the rest of our time together.

Some teachers are not comfortable dealing with concerns they have with students in this manner and prefer instead to let someone else deal with the behaviour so they can continue with the job of teaching. Yes, it was easier for me to find the time because I didn't have the schedule and responsibility of a classroom teacher. As an administrator, I would gladly free up time for anyone who wanted to use this method to build a restorative caring relationship with their students. When we use affective statements that share with the student how we feel rather than point out what they are doing wrong, over time, it will help to build empathy and understanding. Not only will the student's behaviour and attitude change, but what a fantastic model the teacher will have been in showing an alternate, better way of dealing with frustrations and solving problems. When we rely on someone else, an authority to deal with the students with whom we are struggling, we give a couple of different, unintentional messages:

1. You are not worth my time
2. I do not have the skills needed to help you.

Both of these messages undermine classroom learning, behaviour and connection.

The other thing I want to be sure to quickly touch on is the fact that this interaction happened in private. Students will behave in ways they may not otherwise behave in order to save face in front of their peers. There was no need for a power struggle, which was where this situation could easily have gone had I decided I was the boss and he was going to listen to me because I said so. When teachers try to embarrass students in order to get compliance, it generally backfires. No one enjoys being called out in front of others and showing respect and consideration to our students encourages them to do the same, while showing them that you care for them regardless of their behaviour at the time.

Jaxon and I had just barely started to make some headway. He started to increase his reading skills and become more confident in math. The sparkle was back in his eye and he was having fun. His mom moves often, and without warning, Jaxon was gone. I hope wherever he lands, he finds someone who will take time to get to know him, care for him, push him and support him.

Stop and Reflect

- Consider the strategy I shared. Could you see yourself doing this?
- How do you know what questions to ask?
- How do we move beyond managing challenging emotions and behaviour to connect and respond to the underlying needs of the student?

NOTES

_____

_____

_____

_____

_____

_____

_____

_____

_____

_____

_____

_____

_____

_____

_____

_____

_____

_____

_____

_____

_____

_____

Tough cookies are most likely the students
who need communication the most.

Chapter 11

Living the Trauma: Allowing what Happened TO Us BECOME Us

While reading this chapter, I'd like you to consider:

- What is fueling the passion you have?
- Or causing you to behave in certain ways?
- But what happens when the WHY consumes you and becomes your identity?

I want to share with you the story of Jason. Jason's dad was a good ol' all around American boy, captain of the football team in high-school, he volunteered when needed and everyone knew they could count on him. He was kind, considerate, had a great work ethic, loved Jesus and the outdoors. On top of this, he loved his wife and children above all else and he spent his life wanting to be the best dad and husband he could be. When he wasn't at work, he had the family out camping or fishing or exploring some aspect of the natural world.

Unfortunately, a tragic accident took him far too soon, and the entire community was shaken by his death. He left behind a family of four very young children, a broken-hearted wife, sister and brothers. When I met Jason, it was the first day of school in Grade 6. I asked students to please tell me something about themselves or their summer experience they would like to share that first day of school. When I got to Jason, his response startled me. He simply said, "My name is Jason and my dad died six years ago."

When something traumatic happens in a child's life, it changes the way they perceive the world and their place in it. Not only does this trauma-induced view of themselves impact their behaviour, but also their perception of how others see them. It becomes difficult for these children to separate the action or event from themselves and to not internalize it as part of who they are. You see, as kids are growing and developing, they are forming a picture of who they are. They are creating their own identity, looking to find their place in the world. For a student like Jason, suffering a life-altering event at such a critical time of development had caused him to take that in as a piece of *who he was...the kid without a dad.*

Jason never got over losing his dad. His dad was his hero. Every aspect of his life had been and is shadowed by the fact that his dad died. When he struggles with his academics, he says he can't do it because his dad died. When he doesn't get his way or is not included with friends, he says they are mean to him because he has no dad. He uses the same reasoning when he doesn't win a game or excel in sports and he feels people are not playing fair. He has an explosive temper that has been allowed to grow and gain momentum because his dad died. From Jason's perspective, he is the kid in the world who has lost a parent. He struggles to see beyond this and recognize that many children have also suffered a similar loss. This traumatic life experience has become *who he is*, not something that happened to him.

Sometimes our *why* becomes part of our identity. I know we are encouraged to dig deep into our own motivations and see what is actually is driving us, but how often do we share that with kids?

Some students are more challenging to connect with than others. These are most likely the ones who need it the most, the ones who are pushing back so hard because they are afraid of showing who they really are. Being vulnerable equates to being in danger for kids who have experienced trauma. Often, kids go through the day as though nothing is wrong or has happened, interacting normally with their friends. Then under the smallest challenge they may unravel or explode. It's not always predictable. I know this firsthand because I was that kid. I fought back, was disrespectful and disruptive and in general a pain in the teacher's backside, because I was terrified of what they might see if they actually saw me. The things that made me feel unsafe were not predictable and could have been the smallest, seemingly inconsequential things. The pain or fear is sometimes so overwhelming that it is easier to be unpopular, in trouble or left alone than to risk someone getting too close--close enough to maybe be able to hurt you again.

We often refer to these kids as *tough cookies*. That in itself gives you, the person with the greatest opportunity to make connections and change, an excuse for not building that relationship. After all, tough cookies resist, push back, offend and don't want anything to do with you. It's hard work to connect with them and find the marshmallow filling inside.

School may be the one place that is safe for many of our students. This is not to suggest that most of our students live in unsafe environments; rather, it is to be aware of the fact that many, maybe most of our students have experienced some form of trauma in their lives. If you are not familiar with the Adverse Childhood Experience (ACE) quiz, I would highly recommend you take a few moments to familiarize yourself with it. One question to consider is why or what makes school a safe place. We all know the answers, but it is a great reminder to think about. Traumatized kids usually feel unsafe and are on guard or alert for danger all the time. Their brains are always in a state of ready to fight, run away or become invisible (freeze). What makes classrooms and schools safe is having high and consistent expectations for all students, along with high levels of support and caring for each student. We don't need to lower expectations or look the other way when students from rough homes or neighborhoods act out. Rather, we need to up our level of caring and support. Having strict and arbitrary rules only serves to increase trauma reactions in people. Having rules that make sense, are thoughtful and understood serve to calm and reassure students who desperately need to have their brains, bodies and emotions settled.

Stop and Reflect

- Who are your *tough cookies*?
- Have you ever considered that they may have suffered some type of trauma in their lives?
- How do we use our knowledge to help the child to recover from the adverse experiences they may have had before the experiences take a lifelong toll?

NOTES

_____

_____

_____

_____

_____

_____

_____

_____

_____

_____

_____

_____

_____

_____

_____

_____

_____

_____

_____

_____

_____

Don't solve the problem for your students.

Help them find a solution.

Chapter 12

Success versus Survival

While reading this chapter, I'd like you to consider:

- Is there a link between trauma and academic ability?
- Do you ever question the life events of your high achievers?

I am not a researcher and can only speak about my own observations and experiences as an educator. I can also draw on personal experiences in school as I look at my own struggles. I have learned a tremendous amount over the past 25+ years as I have worked with a wide cross section of students and families. Based on what I have seen, as well as learned through a variety of conferences, workshops, courses and personal inquiry, I can tell you without hesitation that kids struggle to learn when they are struggling to survive.

I believe that forming a connection with struggling students is critical to student success.

Most of what is considered good education is often what is best for those kids who have experienced trauma. This includes things such as having a predictable routine and structure in your class, using fair practices when solving problems, setting up clear expectations for assignments and assessments, specific and timely feedback, collaboration and communication, clear learning outcomes, as well as keeping your own baggage at home and not bringing it to work.

As an aside, I can tell you that the kids who have experienced or are in trauma are the best at mirror-neuroning you. They are constantly on the lookout for danger or changes. So, when you come to school in a bad mood for whatever reason or you are not as prepared as you should have been, they immediately pick up on it. This sets off their *spidey senses* that all is not well in class, and more often than not, they will react to it. Chances are they are not even consciously aware of this, as their protective mechanism is working at a subconscious level. Kids are good at reading the room, so when you are off your game, that scares a student who has experienced trauma. They don't feel safe, and we see survival behaviour coming out in all sorts of ways.

By remaining aware of the symptoms of trauma, we can anticipate what may happen before it does. When we anticipate outbursts, reactions and struggles, we create a safe environment around discipline and self-management, and this is good for ALL kids. When you are planning a lesson in math or literacy, you always have to take the students who are struggling into consideration. We make adaptations to your lessons to accommodate those students who need that little bit extra academically in order to be successful. Then why aren't we doing the same for the students who are struggling behaviorally, those students who are, for whatever reason, constantly on high alert?

Ross Green, author of The Explosive Child, tells us that all kids do the best they can. When they don't, we need to look at it as though they are missing some skills. We need to turn our focus away from thinking they are willfully misbehaving to considering what are missing skills they need to be taught. Kids do well if they can, and they want to, so what is standing in their way?

Kids do well if they can!

We need to change our paradigm from believing that kids choose to do well if they want to and recognize that sometimes kids want to do well but don't know how. So instead of trying to get kids to want to do well, what we need to do is take a closer look at and ask ourselves, "hat skill is missing in order for this student to be successful in class or school?"

When we shift our thinking from *kids do well if they want or choose to* and think instead **kids do well if they can**, amazing things happen. Our attitude changes dramatically and we don't view the student as intentionally being a pain in order to mess up our day or plans. Instead, we see the behaviours as a way to detract or survive. The way we see that student changes. The challenge or power struggle no longer needs to exist, because it is not defiance we are dealing with, it is frustration over a missing or undeveloped skill that can be taught, practiced and learned. It is easier to figure out what students need to learn than it is to figure out what is going to motivate them today.

So how do we figure it out or help them?

Make a list of the problems they are having. You cannot even begin to do this without having a positive connection with them. If they don't trust you, they can't learn from you. Once you have a list or know what areas in which they are struggling, you have the insight to determine what the gaps are in their abilities or skill set. This gives you a concrete and real place to start reaching them in a way that will make real and lasting differences. By dissecting their behaviour and seeing that behaviour as a roadmap to identify and discover learning needs, whether social, emotional or academic, you can create a plan for support while maintaining high expectations.

We often say that Amy is making bad choices, or has chosen to misbehave, and if that is her choice, we need to make her see that a different choice is better. We fall into the pattern or habit of punitive consequences or rewards, neither of which actually work. It is difficult to separate the deed from the doer.

Yet with practice we can view others' behaviours as separate from them and as a form of communicating with us.

In light of the conversation we just had about focusing on skill deficits, that way of thinking needs to change. What curious questions can we ask to help uncover the message a behaviour or lack of behaviour may be sending?

I also believe that some student behaviors become habitual or automatic. The sooner you can interrupt that habit in them, the better. What I mean by this is that when we have identified what message the behaviour is conveying and what area of growth or learning needs to take place, the negative actions can be replaced by newly-learned ones. When we as educators are of the mindset that consequences and rewards are required, we miss the golden opportunity for growth and the satisfaction that comes from it. This will be discussed in more depth in a subsequent chapter.

We had a group of students in one cohort who were particularly challenging. We firmly believed in doing whatever needed to be done in order to reach and teach kids. But this group as a whole was testing our patience. In an effort to understand what was going on, we met with each student individually as a team of four or five key people in the school. During the meetings, we asked curious questions. We looked for understanding and clarity from the student's perspective. Some of the things we were curious about were their perspectives on school, what they liked and what they disliked. Who were their friends? What were their hobbies? Did they feel like they belonged, and the teachers liked them? Did they like any of the teachers? We asked how they were doing academically and if they were excited about any projects or things they were learning. We asked if they felt they were struggling with anything.

This gave us a sense of who, if anyone, the student was connected to either currently or in past years. This also gave us a sense of what was missing for them in their school experiences. We always ended the meeting by thanking them for being there and for being brave or courageous enough to share with us. We then asked if there was a person in the building they would like to have as their contact person, the person they felt like having as a touch base, check-in person. We explained it was no big deal, not a homework or behaviour check, but just an overall check in. We also asked if we could meet again next semester. The majority of the time at first, students were hesitant and suspicious of our motives, but they always ended by agreeing to meet with us and by naming an adult in the building who they would like to greet them daily.

Did this process take time? You bet it did.

Did it pay off? Yes, it did.

I would be lying if I claimed that this strategy turned this group around, and we never had another issue with them again. I will not say that. What I will say, however, is that the difference in their behaviour showed a marked improvement. The connection between student and teacher served a two-fold purpose--it made the student know and feel they were seen, understood and appreciated, and it also gave the teacher insight and appreciation for the student. You may not have a team in your school who has the time or ability to do this. That is not stopping you from taking time to get to know those kids with whom you are struggling. Find out what they need and what skills are they missing. If you have behaviour problems in your classroom, you need to dig down and build connection and relationships.

This is an opportunity to model problem-solving with kids. By working collaboratively with them, you are not doing it to them or for them, and you are certainly not ignoring the problem. We need to work **with** them in order to help them learn how to solve their problems, and this cannot be done without a good relationship or connection with a student. We need to have empathy to identify what the concern is and then have a brainstorm session with the student to discover solutions for the problem.

This works with kids of all ages, by the way. Don't solve the problem for them!! Ask them if they have any ideas about how this might be solved. What are some possible solutions? Does this work for everyone involved? If the student comes up with solutions that don't work for you or others, discuss that with them. Explain to them how it doesn't work and the reasons why not. Help them develop and see flexibility in problem-solving in order to come up with a plan that works for everyone. So often we as adults are unsure of how to move past the behaviour to the source or cause. We may be unskilled ourselves, having no idea where to even begin. Start by building a connection that will help you to uncover what is really going on that is preventing the student from being successful.

So, is there a link between trauma and academic ability? I would say yes, most definitely.

Stop and Reflect:
- Can you think of any students, past or present, that may benefit from going through a process similar to this?
- What might those benefits be?
- How could you facilitate this process?

NOTES

Something as small as a high five or a quick word of appreciation or thanks is key to a student's success.

Chapter 13

This Entitled Generation

While reading this chapter, I'd like you to consider:

- How often have you thought or said, "these kids are so entitled"?
- Where does the entitled behaviour stem from?

When I heard the boys were once again in my office waiting for me, I shook my head in disbelief. Hadn't I created a plan for them just yesterday? I cannot tell you the countless times I have had these three particular boys in my office. Each time the story was more or less the same with just a slight change in the details.

Lance is hot-tempered and unable to see past his self-perceived injustices. I have lost track of how many times he has been in my office. He seems to have no ability to regulate his own emotions or see the world from any perspective other than his own. He has grown up overly-protected due to a serious and traumatizing childhood sickness. To say he has been excessively loved (by some definitions spoiled) is an understatement. He was raised by grandparents who were his number one advocates!

You have met Ichabod in an earlier chapter, an introvert with a soft heart and voice. He and his siblings remind me of beaten, hungry puppies. They don't look you in the eye except for occasional glances, they skitter around with their heads down and stay just out of reach. He has witnessed and been affected by more violence in a lifetime than anyone should. He is an outcast from his class and a misfit both behaviourally and physically. His clothes are often dirty and too small. He wears the same thing day in and day out and is always hungry. Ichabod also has a quick and aggressive temper. It often comes out of nowhere and it's hard to help him work through it.

Like Ichabod, Liam is also a very shy, soft-spoken boy. However, unlike Ichabod, he comes from a traditional family unit of two parents and two brothers. He has a classic stay-at-home mom who walks him and his brothers to school and every day and dad is there to pick them up. He has bikes, a dog and a dad who spends time playing with him. Liam struggles with academics and talks with a lisp. His mom is determined to create a good life for her boys and is a strong advocate for them. To say she assertively insists that their needs are met would be accurate.

The boys had been getting along well in the past, meaning they hadn't been in my office for some time, except for the day before when we'd reviewed the plans they had made regarding how to get along.

It is important to have regular check-ins with students who frequently struggle.

That way you can reinforce some of their positive behaviours by identifying them and going through necessary questions when they are calm and happy. It is also important to acknowledge and connect when things are going well. Something as small as a high five or a quick word of appreciation or thanks is key to their success. It is important not only to catch kids struggling and talk to them then, but to catch them on a great day and reinforce the correct behaviour. This was why I was disappointed to see they were back today.

It seems there were some issues around the game they had been playing. Ichabod, who lives in a world where gaming is the most important thing, had changed the rules of the game. He'd tried to 'level up,' so to speak, and had make the game more complex and difficult than it had been. He often took online experiences and tried to recreate them on the playground or classroom. That is an entirely different chapter, if not a book, we can explore later.

Needless to say, the other boys were tired of playing a real-life game where they didn't understand the rules and the rules seemed to keep changing. So, the argument was on. As usual, it was two boys against one.

As I went through the questions about what had happened and what were they thinking, as well as who had been impacted and how they could resolve this issue, I was genuinely struck by Liam's response. While the other two boys seemed to want to solve the problem, I was unsure if Liam even wanted to do so. His defense for the way he'd treated Ichabod was that Ichabod annoyed him.

To say I was floored would be an understatement. He genuinely believed that because he was annoyed, he was allowed to be rude, hurtful and downright mean. His lack of empathy and understanding could and would be labeled as entitlement by many. I saw it as a lack of connection and understanding. He was missing the ability to see how his actions, words and attitude were contributing to the problem.

When we allow children to grow up believing they are the only people who matter, we do them such a disservice. Providing opportunities for reaching out and helping others allows and teaches them how important our interactions are, builds empathy and communicates a sense of social responsibility.

I am bothered when people talk about how entitled this generation is. I perceive it as the fact that the younger generations have a different value system than I do and that perhaps my lack of understanding their values or moral code leads to discomfort on my part. I understand entitlement in its purest form--when a person wants their own way and in fact believes their needs, wishes or desires are more important than those of others. There are those who have no sense of the needs or feelings of other human beings. The entitlement to which I'm referring is the view this generation seems to have on how the world should be. It is easier to label something or someone than to explore the reasons or unspoken issues that are driving that lack of comfort or understanding. If we truly desire to impact change in our students, in the world and in those we interact with and care for, we need to seek to understand, rather than judge and label.

Stop and Reflect

- Is expecting that the world owes you, or revolves around your entitlement?

- What is the missing piece? What skill is missing?

- How do we overcome "entitlement?"

- Is what we have labeled as entitled really a lack of empathy?

NOTES

It takes courage to get up when you have fallen,

failed or been knocked down.

Chapter 14

Building Resilience with Courage

While reading this chapter, I'd like you to consider:

- Be honest...How many times have you forgotten you asked that kid to sit out in the hall?
- Is removing kids from the classroom the easy way out?

The kids who enter our rooms are ours. They are there for the year and it is up to us to teach them. We need to do everything we can, to keep them in our classroom and in our school. So often, it is difficult to keep the student that disrupts our lesson in the class, it is easier to ask them to sit in the hall and think about their behaviour. When that doesn't work, the next step is inevitably to send them to the office. Our schools have a set of rules or a policy for dealing with students who continuously disrupt the learning of other students. These eventually lead to suspensions, part-time programs or worse.

Educators have to wear so many different hats in order to help become kids ready to learn from them. We have students coming into our classroom with a variety of baggage, from broken homes, to abuse and neglect. We have students coming to our classes hungry, tired, worried, scared and worse. We have kids who come fed, clean, loved, and eager to learn.

I recall participating in an activity where I was asked to identify the various hats I wore throughout the day or week, to colour code them and to identify the need I filled while wearing each of those hats. The reality is that students come to us from where they are, and our job is ultimately to teach them. We need to be okay with the fact that many of them are struggling, traumatized and reacting to circumstances mostly beyond our control. It is up to us to provide a safe environment so a healthy connection can grow.

Resilience is the ability to move forward, bounce back and continue to grow or learn after life has knocked us down or we have endured a setback. It is the ability not to give up, to keep going regardless of what life gives us.

So, how do we teach children, who are in fact just babies, to be resilient?

How do we teach them not to give up when things are bad or not fair and they have no idea what is going to happen, when all they want to do is be safe and seen? We set up structures and offer support though examples of what this means. We give them opportunities to show and understand their ability to be resilient. We explain what resilience is. We share ideas of resilience and recognize when they are practicing resiliency. Explain it, practice it, see it, name it and celebrate it! Be transparent and explicit. When we explain what resiliency is, why it's important and how to be resilient, kids are more likely to practice those skills that will help to develop it. Don't hope or expect that students, especially those who are struggling, will understand what it is and why it's important. Many times, people are too discouraged by life circumstances, or they have never seen what resilience looks like. I have been in classes where they intentionally teach self-regulation, and they talk about it openly. Do the same with resilience. One of my favourite teachers used to say, "If you don't paint the bullseye, how do you expect them to hit it? "

If we don't define resiliency, how can we expect students to understand how to become resilient?

I think there is a common misconception that we are either born with resilience or we aren't. There is some truth to this. Some people do have the natural ability to be resilient more than others. I believe that this is much more environmental than it is biological. We are taught resiliency in some way. As we experience success, we become more and more resilient.

*If you are interested in learning more, just Google the **resilience scale**.*

It takes courage to work with and love students with a trauma-affected background, to help them develop resilience and move past the effects of these events. It takes courage on your part to work with these most needy students, to see them and use their experiences to help them grow. It has been scientifically shown that the more positive experiences people have, the more trusting relationships, the more positive learning experiences, along with increased responsibility and a safe environment, the more apt they are to develop the skills and abilities that in turn strengthen resilience.

One of the first things that is needed is to ensure that our classrooms and schools are safe places to take risks and are free from judgement, ridicule, and social punishment. Schools should be a place where individual strengths and interests are valued. When we are free to make mistakes and learn from those mistakes, we are learning, but even better, we are becoming more resilient. If you are familiar with John Hattie's work on **Visible Learning,** you understand the importance of being crystal clear about expectations, offering specific and constructive feedback and assessing for growth and learning. As an aside, if you are not familiar with John Hattie's work, I strongly suggest you take a look at it, it has changed student success rates in many districts.

When these structures are in place, students know what is expected and what they can expect. It is helpful to ensure that there is some student voice and input in the classroom and even schoolwide expectations. Teachers who intentionally and specifically teach resilience are changing students' outlook and opportunities in life. Instead of being defeated by setbacks or failure, students learn how to make that failure temporary and use it to learn.

Resilience is the ability to overcome negative experiences and to recover from them and move on. How we process, react to and respond to negative experiences or events helps develop and grow our resilience. Children need to have this ability taught to and modeled for them. As educators, one of the most impactful things we can help our students learn is how to be resilient. We all know those students who are sooo discouraged about the fact that they are less than 100% in their academics. I have tried to help them come to realize that if they already know everything, they are not learning anything. We need to help students understand the process of learning, how they learn and to see 'mistakes' not as mistakes but as things that still need to be learned.

Resilience is a mindset that is strengthened through experiences. Children need to have us show them how to change the way they think so they can impact their life circumstances and to overcome whatever life may throw at them. When we connect in a meaningful way with students, when we are able to be the safe place for them to learn and understand, when we are clear about our expectations, rules and routines, when we model learning from our own mistakes and are able to be appropriately vulnerable with our students, we are showing them how to become resilient.

We are giving them the tools they need to know that they are not stuck in their circumstances, but can in fact rise above them, overcome and choose a better path for themselves. We do this by breaking big tasks down into bite-sized, manageable chunks, by encouraging and modeling reflection on our learning and planning next steps, facing small challenges and identifying how we overcame them. When students believe they are worthy and capable of overcoming challenges, they become resilient.

It takes courage to get up when you have fallen, failed or been knocked down.

It takes courage to try again. Celebrate that courage! You cannot teach resilience if you do not have a connection. In all the research, theory, and available techniques, it all comes back to connection and relationship. If you want to reach kids and give them all the knowledge you have to offer them, you first need to connect with them. You first need to give them your attention and get to know them before you can teach.

It sounds so simple. It is not a new concept by any means. I am asking you to have the courage needed to connect with students who are resisting you with whom you don't particularly want to connect, and I am asking you to be intentional and vulnerable with your students. There is an intentionality on your part which must be present. Eventually, I promise it becomes easier and more natural as you interact with your students.

Stop and Reflect

- How do you become intentional in creating connections?
- What clues and cues are you going to use to help form meaningful relationships and connections?

NOTES

Final Thoughts

I deeply believe in the transformation that comes not only to the individual, but the family, school and community, when relationships and connectivity are part of school culture. I have experienced firsthand the tremendous impact putting people first can have in a work environment, restoring a once-toxic environment to a peaceful, positive, collaborative, empathetic and loving workplace. These experiences transcend to our students, and in so doing have lasting and deeply transformative effects on our community.

In an effort to genuinely make a difference in the world, I have shared these stories with you in the hopes that they have touched your heart and helped to reaffirm what you know about the importance of connecting in real and authentic ways with our students.

It is my deep belief that the only way we truly can make a difference in our classrooms, schools and future generations is to build and teach communities to be empathetic and caring, and to nurture the human connection. It is my wish that all members of the community hold that at the forefront when making decisions and problem-solving.

The first professional development I participated in that focused on building empathy, relationships and connection significantly shifted my perspective. I intentionally changed the way I interacted with others both at work and at home. Through understanding and practicing empathy and intentionality, I was able to impact students, teachers, parents and family as I had not been able to before.

There is no question that when we, as educators, leaders, and impactors, recognize the significance of our interactions with others and are able to align our actions with that understanding, sustainable change can and will happen. The steps are simple and straightforward and allow for our hearts and minds to align with what is best for kids.

It is my hope that these stories will inspire you to try again, to see the students with whom you are struggling to relate in a whole new light.

If you are interested in exploring how you can create a trauma-informed, connected school, reach out to me.

You can visit my website: www.margotmckinley.com, **or you can find me on Facebook: Phase III with Margot McKinley**

**Link for free workbook – To obtain the free "how to" companion workbook visit margotmckinley.com

Works Cited:

Bessel Van der Kolk MD, Sean Pratt, et al. (2014). The Body Keeps the Score: Brain, Mind, and Body in the Healing of Trauma. https://www.cdc.gov/violenceprevention/childabuseandneglect/acestudy/index. html

Bruce Perry, Maia Szalavitz, et al. (2006)
The Boy Who Was Raised as a Dog: And Other Stories from a Child Psychiatrist's

Notebook - What Traumatized Children Can Teach Us About Loss, Love, and Healing

Costello, B., Wachtel, J., Wachtel, T. (2013). IIRP The Restorative Practices Handbook: For Teachers, Disciplinarians and Administrators.

Costello, B., Wachtel, J., Wachtel, T. (2013). Restorative Circles in Schools: Building Community and Enhancing Learning

Craig, S. (2015) Trauma Sensitive Schools

Green, R. (1998). The Explosive Child: A New Approach for Understanding and Parenting Easily Frustrated, Chronically Inflexible Children

Romero, V., Robertson, R., Warner, A. (2018) Building Resilience in Students Impacted by Adverse Childhood Experiences: A Whole Staff Approach.

Schuster, K. (2020). https://childmind.org/article/classroom-anxiety-in-children/
Smith, D., Fisher, D., et. al. (2015). Better Than Carrots or Sticks: Restorative Practices for

Positive Classroom Management

Souers, K., Hall P. (2016). Fostering Resilient Learners: Strategies for Creating a Trauma-Sensitive Classroom

Waack, S. (2020). Visible Learning https://visible-learning.org/john-hattie/

Weldon G. (2020). https://lauragraceweldon.com/2019/09/15/benevolent-childhood-experiences/

CPSIA information can be obtained
at www.ICGtesting.com
Printed in the USA
LVHW060022030623
748642LV00016B/1690